A GUIDE TO THE INDIAN MINIATURE

© National Museum, Janpath, New Delhi
First Edition, 1994
Second Edition, 1997
Editor: R.R.S. Chauhan
Layout and Design: Kushal Pal
Production: Sanjib Kumar Singh

Price Rs. 105/-
Sole Distributors
Publications Division, Patiala House, New Delhi

Published by National Museum, Janpath, New Delhi
Printed by S. Narayan & Sons, New Delhi

ISBN 81-85832-01-3

A Guide to the
Indian Miniature

Pramod Ganpatye

 National Museum, Janpath, New Delhi

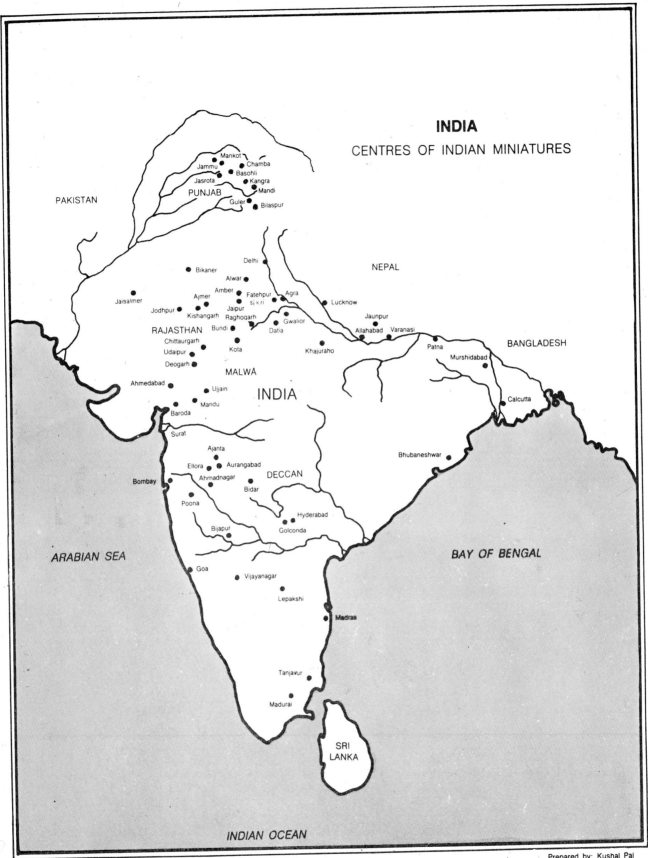

INDIA

CENTRES OF INDIAN MINIATURES

PAKISTAN

Mankot
Jammu • • Chamba
Basohli
Jasrota • • Kangra
PUNJAB • Mandi
Guler • • Bilaspur

Bikaner • Delhi
Alwar •
Amber • • Fatehpur
Ajmer • Si k ri
Jodhpur • Jaipur
Kishangarh • Raghogarh
RAJASTHAN Bundi •
Chittaurgarh •
Udaipur •
Kota •
Deogarh •
MALWA
Ahmedabad •
Ujjain •
Mandu •
Baroda •
Surat •

Agra •
Lucknow •
Gwalior • Jaunpur •
Datia • Allahabad • Varanasi •
Khajuraho •
Patna •
Murshidabad •
Calcutta •

NEPAL

BANGLADESH

INDIA

Ajanta •
Ellora • • Aurangabad
Ahmadnagar
Bombay • Bidar • DECCAN
Poona •
Bijapur •
Hyderabad •
Golconda •

Bhubaneshwar •

ARABIAN SEA

Goa •
Vijayanagar •
Lepakshi •

Madras •

BAY OF BENGAL

Tanjavur •

Madurai •

SRI
LANKA

INDIAN OCEAN

Prepared by: Kushal Pal

ACKNOWLEDGEMENT

This small guide has been written by me for the visitors at the instance of late Dr. L.P. Sihare, former Director General, National Museum, New Delhi.

Shri Karl J. Khandalavala, a distinguished art historian, was kind enough to go through the manuscript. I am greatly indebted to him for his kind guidance and learned comments.

My heartiest thanks are due to Shri R.R.S. Chauhan, Keeper (Publications), late S.B. Mathur (Production Officer), Shri Kushal Pal (Layout Artist), and Shri Sanjib Kumar Singh (Technical Assistant) for their earnest efforts to bring out this publication. Without their active co-operation and help, this work would not have seen the light of the day. I also thank Shri V.T. Pillai for typing the manuscript.

Lastly, I express my sincere gratitude to Dr. R.C. Sharma, Director General, National Museum for extending me all the facilities in its completion.

– Pramod Ganpatye

SECOND EDITION

This is a reprint of the first edition of the Guide. I express my sincere gratitude to the present Director General, National Museum, Dr. S.S. Biswas, for extending all facilities for its publication.

New Delhi   – Pramod Ganpatye

Dated : May 23, 1997

INDIAN MINIATURE PAINTING

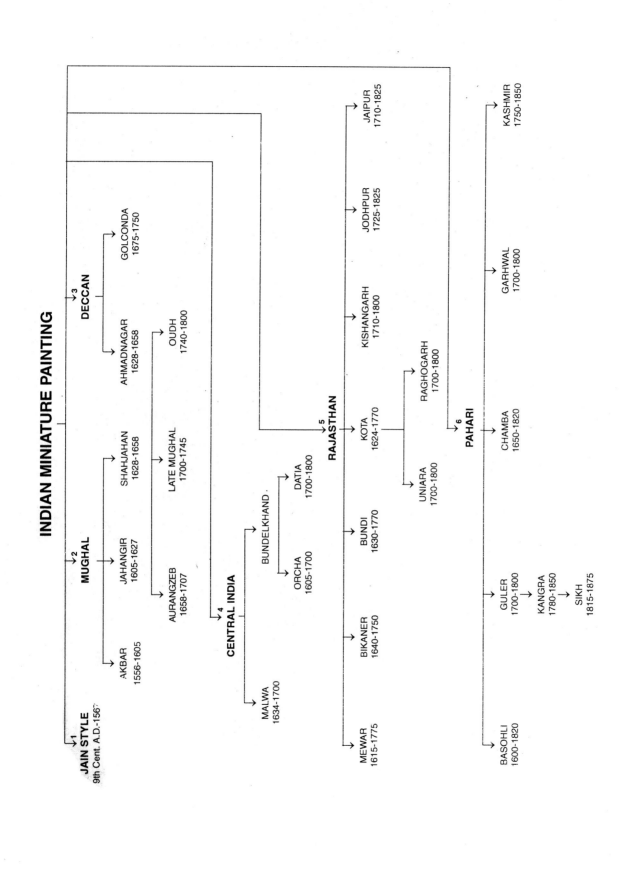

JAIN STYLE
9th Cent. A.D.-1567

→1

→2 **MUGHAL**

AKBAR
1556-1605

JAHANGIR
1605-1627

SHAHJAHAN
1628-1658

AURANGZEB
1658-1707

LATE MUGHAL
1700-1745

→3 **DECCAN**

AHMADNAGAR
1628-1658

GOLCONDA
1675-1750

OUDH
1740-1800

→4 **CENTRAL INDIA**

MALWA
1634-1700

BUNDELKHAND

ORCHA
1605-1700

DATIA
1700-1800

→5 **RAJASTHAN**

MEWAR
1615-1775

BIKANER
1640-1750

BUNDI
1630-1770

KOTA
1624-1770

UNIARA
1700-1800

RAGHOGARH
1700-1800

KISHANGARH
1710-1800

JODHPUR
1725-1825

JAIPUR
1710-1825

→6 **PAHARI**

BASOHLI
1600-1820

GULER
1700-1800

KANGRA
1780-1850

SIKH
1815-1875

CHAMBA
1650-1820

GARHWAL
1700-1800

KASHMIR
1750-1850

INTRODUCTION

The art of painting has been a medium of both expression and communication from the earliest known period of history. Man, as nomad, wandering in search of food and security, gradually discovered a language of line and form for expressing his ideas; which account for pre-historic paintings appearing in rock shelters. At a later period, this found expression in the paintings on chalcolithic pottery discovered at various centres. In India, the patterns were either geometric or were styled after the flora and fauna and at times depicted human figures.

The art of painting in India progressed gradually and it reached its zenith during the Satavahana period (2nd-1st B.C.) and also the Gupta-Vakataka period (5th-6th A.D.). Mainly of the Buddhist theme, the paintings were on the large canvas of granite walls of the Ajanta caves. The style was line-oriented and natural, besides being brilliant in colour. The painters drew inspiration from the legends related to the previous incarnations of Buddha.

The pattern of large scale wall painting which had dominated the scene, witnessed the advent of miniature paintings during the 11th & 12th centuries. This new style figured first in the form of illustrations etched on palm-leaf manuscripts. The contents of these manuscripts included literature on the Buddhism and Jainism. In eastern India, the principle centres of artistic and intellectual activities of the Buddhist religion were Nalanda, Odantapuri, Vikramshila and Somarupa situated in the Pala kingdom (Bengal and Bihar). Buddhist works like the **Ashtasahasrika-Prajnaparamita**, the **Mahamayuri** and the **Pancharaksha** are few examples to cite, which were illustrated with Buddhist deities in late Ajanta style. In western India, however, it was the Jain faith which dominated, Rajasthan, Gujarat and Malwa being the principle centres of Jain religion and art. Apart from the **Kalkacharya Katha** and the **Kalpasutra**, two well-known Jain treatises, Hindu themes such as the **Balagopal Stuti** as well as secular works like the **Vasanta Vilas** found expression on palm-leaf illustrations and came to be known as the Jain or Western Indian Style of painting. The Jain Style is unique as it bears an exaggerated linear quality. Facial outlines are emphasized, the nose is long and sharp, and the eyes are shaped like petals with the farther eye projected beyond the outline of the face (Page 36). The backgrounds are illuminated in shades of dark blue, red and green or yellow. Gold is used for decorative purpose, especially in the manuscripts of a later era, which were done on paper, a medium, that had replaced the palm-leaf.

In these the compositional format is confined to figures or objects generally arranged in horizontal bands.

It was in the 14th century A.D. that paper replaced the palm-leaf. The Jain Style of paintings attained a high degree of development by the late 15th and early 16th century. A new trend in manuscript illustration was set by a manuscript of the **Nimatnama** painted at Mandu, during the reign of Nasir Shah (1500-1510 A.D.). This represented a synthesis of the indigenous and the Persian Style, though it was the latter which dominated the Mandu manuscripts. There was another style of painting known as Lodi Khuladar that flourished in the Sultanate's dominion of North India extending from Delhi to Jaunpur during the late 15th and early 16th century. The best known example of the Lodi Style is the famous **Aranyaka Parvan** belonging to the Asiatic Society, Bombay painted in 1516 A.D. during the victorious reign of Sikandar Shah Lodi at Kachuvava, about 57 miles away from Agra. Fine specimens of paintings in Jaur Style can be seen in the well-known manuscripts such as the **Chaura Panchashika** and the **Gita-Govinda**. This style is marked by the ornaments adorning the women and their pendulous breasts, besides the chequered designs of their garments (Page 37). The figures have large eyes and exaggerated profiles. Though emanating from the Jain Style of Delhi and Jaunpur, this form has striking characteristics of its own.

Akbar's reign (1556-1605) ushered a new era in Indian miniature painting. He was the first monarch who established in India an atelier under the supervision of two Persian master-artists, Mir Sayyed Ali and Abdul-ul-Samad Khan. Earlier, both of them had served under the patronage of Humayun in Kabul and accompanied him to India when he regained his throne in 1555. Later, a number of artists were engaged to work under their guidance to decorate Akbar's imperial studio at Fatehpur Sikri. One of the first productions of that school of painting was the **Hamzanama** series, which, according to the court historian, Badayuni, was started in 1567 and completed in 1582. It is interesting to note that most of the artists belonged to the Hindu communities hailing from Gujarat, Gwalior and Kashmir, who gave birth to a new school of painting, popularly known as the Mughal School of Painting. This synthesis of the Saffavid School and the indigenous *kalams* of miniature art, owes a debt to the secular outlook of Akbar. And it proved to be a landmark in the history of Indian miniature painting. Akbar commissioned a large number of manuscripts, illustrated in this style, for his Imperial Library. However, this style of painting reached its zenith during the reigns of Jahangir (1605-1627) and Shah Jahan (1628-1658), but declined rapidly during the years that followed under the rule of Aurangzeb (1658-1707).

The earliest known manuscript illustrated in this fashion during Akbar's regime is the **Duwal-Rani-Khizar-Khani.** Written by the celebrated poet Amir Khusro, the illustrations are attributed to Mir Sayyed Ali, the master-painter, who undertook the work in 1568. The paintings of the **Hamzanama** which represented the most ambitious project undertaken during the golden era of Akbar, were executed on large canvas made of cotton cloth. Initially, the work was started by about 30 artists, but their number grew to more than a hundred at the time of its completion. The work on these illustrations served as an excellent training ground for the painters of the royal atelier. The style of Mughal paintings is distinguished by the dramatic action and bold brush work. Apart from the **Hamzanama,** many other manuscripts such as the **Razmanama,** the **Baburnama,** the **Akbarnama** etc., were also illustrated in similar vein.

It was in the last quarter of the 16th century that European influence began to affect the Mughal School. Hence, a number of Christian themes were also painted by the Mughal artists. Jahangir was an enthusiastic patron of the arts. He possessed an innate quality for the appreciation of painting and talent for observing the nature keenly. Whenever he came across an unusual plant or bird or animal, he instructed his artists to paint them. Particularly, Mansur, one of the most talented painters, excelled in animal and bird motifs. The art of painting attracted and charmed Jahangir so much that his period is remarkable for beautiful illustrations of several manuscripts. Jahangir's period is characterised by naturalism, both in colour and form. During Shah Jahan's reign (1628-1658), the Mughal artists' favourite themes for paintings were emperors and princes visiting Sufi saints. In addition, court scenes, portraits and studies of birds and animals continued to be depicted.

The fine quality of the Mughal painting was sustained during the period of Shah Jahan, even though he paid greater attention to architecture. The high quality work of the earlier reigns did not survive during the period of Aurangzeb, although some good portraiture and hunting scenes were executed in his time. Being an orthodox Muslim, he did not encourage the art of painting. However, in the reigns of Farrukhsyiar (1713-1719) and Muhammed Shah (1719-1748), the art of miniature painting was revived again. A known romantic as Muhammad Shah was, love scenes and romantic subjects began to feature frequently, which seemed to rebound on Aurangzeb's puritanical attitude.

The era of Mughal painting came to an end during the period of Shah Alam (1759-1806) when the Mughal empire was virtually confined to an area enclosed by the walls of the Red Fort in Delhi.

The style of paintings in the provincial cities of the Mughal empire such as Murshidabad, Faizabad, Lucknow and Patna has been described as Provincial Mughal. The Mughal Governors of these provinces had assumed independent status following the decline of Mughal empire during the middle of the 18th century. There were no drastic changes in the Provincial Mughal Style of painting, but it has certain recognisable features of its own. Mir Chand was one of the best known artists of this period. Other provincial artists sought to imitate earlier work to suit the varying tastes of their patrons rather than evolving distinctive styles of their own.

As for the Deccani painting, initially it was a product of the Sheraz Style of Persian painting and the local art forms of the Hindu kingdom of Vijayanagar. Later, it was influenced by the Mughal Style during the late 17th and 18th century. The earliest surviving examples of Deccani painting go back to circa A.D. 1565-1567 and are now scattered in many collections belonging to Ahmadnagar and Bijapur Schools. A school of Deccani painting also flourished at Golconda, the style of which is remarkably consistent in quality and is a combination of a high degree of technical excellence with refinement of line and a subtle richness in its colour palette.

The Bijapur School of painting was patronized and developed under the powerful king Ali Adil Shah I (1558-1580) and his successor, Ibrahim Adil Shah II (1580-1627), a great lover of art. An illustrated manuscript of the **Nujum-ul-ulum,** a book on astronomy which was painted at Bijapur during 1580, is the most notable work of the early Bijapur School. Prior to this, the **Tarif-i-Husain Shahi** manuscript was written and illustrated at Ahmadnagar during 1565-1567. The Golconda School commenced under Ibrahim in the middle of the 17th century and continued till the period of Abdullah Qutub Shah (1626-1672) and last Golconda ruler Tana Shah (1672-1687). The style of this school was distinguished by rich colours, considerable use of gold and the frequent use of unusual architectural forms. The art of painting in the Deccan continued till late 18th century but it became increasingly decorative. However, there are some fine sets of the **Ragamala,** which were painted during 1725-1778.

Rajasthani paintings covered a wide area including Malwa, Bundelkhand, Mewar, Bundi, Kota, Jaipur, Bikaner, Sirohi, Sawar, Kishangarh and Marwar. What is interesting to note is that each centre developed its own individual characteristics. In Rajputana, painting was already in vogue in the form of Western Indian or Jain Style. This had provided a base for the growth of various schools of painting under the influence of popular Mughal School from circa 1590-1600. Nevertheless, the Rajasthani *kalams* developed their own styles in the years that followed.

The earliest available set of Rajasthani painting is the **Ragamala** done by a Muslim artist, Nissardin, in 1605 at Chawand in Mewar. Yet another **Ragamala** in the Mewar Style was painted by the artist Sahibdin in 1628. Sahibdin's work greatly influenced the development of early Rajasthani painting in Mewar. He became the principle artist of the Mewar court during the reign of Jagat Singh I (1628-1652).

The rise of Vaisnavism and the Bhakti cult in Rajasthan exercised a marked influence both on literature and pictorial art. Krishna became the supreme god, while Radha was considered as the symbol of divine love.

Most of the themes in art and literature revolved largely around them. The famous literary and poetic works such as the **Gita-Govinda** written by the court poet Jay Deva who lived in Bengal in the 12th century; the **Rasikapriya** by Kesava Das of Orcha (1555-1617); the **Amaru Shataka,** the hundred love lyrics by Amaru; Bihari's Satsai (circa 1603-1663), the classification of its heroes and heroines theme, better known as the **Nayika Bheda,** were repeatedly illustrated with these forms. Apart from mythological stories, the **Devi Purana,** the **Bhagavata Purana,** the **Ramayana,** the **Mahabharata,** the **Ragamala,** the **Baramasa** and the activities of daily life were extensively painted.

One striking feature of Rajasthani painting is the arrangement of figures as even small figures are not obscured in the composition. The background, the flora and fauna and the symbols help the composition to express an intensity of feelings and emotions. Architecture usually painted in the background, is used as a device to create perspective and depth. Faces are often modelled with a tinge of colour to impart a certain roundness to them. In the 18th century, the names of rulers, artists and even dates and titles sometimes appear on the upper margin of the paintings. Foremost amongst the Rajasthani schools are those of Mewar, Malwa, Jaipur, Jodhpur, Nagaur, Sirohi, Kota, Bundi, Bikaner and Kishangarh, while many *thikanas* (feudal baronies) such as Deogarh, Ghanerao, Malpura, Pali etc. also had painters at their own courts.

The Malwa Style is marked by bold and strong colours. Figures with long wide eyes are usually projected against monochrome backgrounds of varying rich tonalities. The composition are very simple and the picture space is often divided into compartments in order to separate one scene from the other. An important series of paintings in the Malwa Style is a **Rasikapriya** dated 1634, which was certainly painted in Orcha. There are also illustrations in the **Ramayana** and the **Bhagavata Purana** and there are good reasons to believe that they were painted about 1642-1645 for the queen, Hira Rani, wife of Pahar Singh of Orcha. An **Amaru Shataka** series was painted in circa 1652 at Nasaratgarh near Mandu, while a **Ragamala** series (now in the National Museum) was painted at Narsinghagarh by an artist named Madhav Das.

Paintings from Mewar assume a great variety for the use of a wide range of colours such as saffron, yellow, ochre, navy blue, brown, crimson, etc. The backgrounds usually have stylised architecture consisting of domed pavilions and small turrets. The treatment of trees is only partially naturalistic, and the foregrounds are decorated with flowers and birds. The menfolk sport a *jama,* a long garment which is both plain and fullskirted. A scarf is worn over one shoulder and sometimes around the waist as well. The turban is either loosely wound or has a band tied tightly around it (Page 44).

Marwar was an important centre of Gujarati-Jain art activities. It was at Marwar and other places such as Jodhpur, Pali and Nagaur that a variety of sub-schools of painting developed during 17th-19th centuries. Of these, Jodhpur is the most important centre of the Marwar School of painting. The turban seen in Marwar painting has its own characteristics. It is funnel-shaped and markedly high (Page 46). The faces are usually drawn in profile, and bright colours are preferred in the composition. Spiral clouds are also shown streaming on the horizon. A large number of portraits, court scenes and themes such as **Baramasa** are to be found in the Jodhpur Style. Though paintings at Pali, a *thikana*, belonging to the Marwar School are somewhat traditional, yet they are important to the art historians for there is a dated **Ragamala** series of 1623 painted by an artist Viraji, several folios of which are now in the National Museum. In Nagaur, another centre of the Marwar School, we find among other subjects several important portraits executed in a markedly dignified style.

Bikaner was one of the most important states of Rajasthan. This state was established in the 15th century by a chieftain named Bika. It was during the middle of the 17th century that a few artists from the Mughal School visited Bikaner and worked there under its patronage. Ali Raza, an *Ustad* (master-painter) from Delhi was amongst them. The names of some other well-known Bikaner artists are Ruknuddin and his son Sahibdin, Isa, Mohammed Ibrahim and Lupha. Most of the Bikaner artists were Muslim, and they worked in a style which although markedly Mughal in character, had certain distinctive features of its own. The Bikaner Style is known for its very fine draughtsmanship and subdued colour tonalities.

The Bundi School came into existence during the early 17th century; an early influence was the popular Mughal Style of a **Ragamala** series painted at Chunar near Banaras in 1591. An example of the early Chunar series, **Bhairon Ragini,** is housed in the Allahabad Museum and there are examples in other collections also. Originally mistaken as a Bundi series, it is in fact a popular Mughal series which influenced the early Bundi School for the Chunar series had come into the possession of a family of Bundi-Kota artists sometimes about 1625-1630 and was used as a model for painting scroll in Bundi and its sister state Kota. It was the influence of the Chunar series that brought into existence the Bundi School. The Bundi School was also influenced by the Deccani painting to some extent. The Bundi artists had their own standard in depicting feminine beauty: women are portrayted with small round faces, receding foreheads, prominent noses and full cheeks, while the female dress usually consists of a *pyjama* over which a transparent *Jama* is worn. Another feature of the Bundi School is lush landscapes painted in vibrant colours and massed with a variety of forms of trees and floral creepers, water ponds with lotus flowers in the foreground, fish and birds. Sometimes a yellow band appears on top of the painting with a text in *Nagiri* characters.

Kota state in the southern Rajasthan was separated from its sister state of Bundi in 1624. The Kota School is so close to the Bundi School that at times it is difficult to assert whether a painting is of the Bundi or the Kota *kalam.* Though a distinctive Kota Style evolved in mid-17th century, similarities between Bundi and Kota painting continued in many respects with discernible variations in details, costumes and methods of shading the faces. The Kota hunting scenes, depicting princes and nobles with their retinue engaged in hunting lions and tigers in the rocky and somewhat sparsely wooded forests of that region, are now world famous.

It was at Amber, the former capital city of Rajasthan, that the Jaipur School of painting originated. The capital was shifted to the newly planned city of Jaipur only in 1728. The rulers at Amber had maintained cordial relations with the Mughal emperors, and this association left its impact on the artistic activities at Amber. Jaipur paintings are plentiful and embrace a variety of subjects, but they neither possess the subtler qualities as evidenced in the Bundi, Kota, Kishangarh or Bikaner Schools nor bear the bolder qualities of Mewar and Marwar Schools of Rajasthani painting.

The state of Kishangarh was founded by Kishan Singh, a younger brother of Raja Sur Singh of Jodhpur in circa 1609. It was during the second quarter of the 18th century (1735-1748) that some of the most charming pieces of Kishangarh painting were produced. Raja Sawant Singh was on the throne during that period. A great patron of art and literature as he was, he composed devotional songs in praise of Radha and Krishna using the pseudonym of Nagari Das.

Kishangarh painting, at its finest, is distinguished by its exquisite quality not to be found in other Rajasthani schools and a distinctive type of female face with receding forehead, arched eyebrows, lotus shaped eyes slightly tinged with pink, sharp pointed nose, thin and sensitive lips and pointed chin. Nihal Chand was the most important artist of Kishangarh, who is said to have worked there between 1735-1757 and probably even later. He executed beautiful portraits of Krishna and Radha, the facial type for Radha being based on the exquisite countenance of Sawant Singh's beloved mistress popularly known as **Bani Thani.** Krishna's face in these paintings was also stylised to look somewhat similar, though as a male countenance to the stylised face of **Bani Thani.** A statement made by some writers that the stylised Kishangarh Radha was not based on the face of **Bani Thani** is due to their ignorance of a tradition believed over two centuries by well-known scholars of Hindi Brij Bhasa. In fact, there is a contemporary painting of her approaching Sawant Singh who is performing *Puja,* and it is also evident that the stylised Kishangarh Radha is based on the tall beautiful figure and face of **Bani Thani** as seen in this painting. Those who opine that these paintings are of a later date appear to be rather ignorant of the stylistic features of Kishangarh paintings.

The art of miniature painting in the Punjab hills known as Pahari painting was influenced to some extent by the Mughal painting of Aurangzeb's period as well as paintings from Nepal, probably via Kashmir, particularly in its stylised tree forms. Pahari paintings had its beginning under Raja

13

Kripal Pal of Basohli (1678-1731), a literary minded ruler who was also a great devotee of Vishnu.

This school has many styles and sub-styles as these paintings developed at various centres such as Basohli, Guler, Chamba, Tehri, Garhwal, Nurpur, Mankot, Mandi, Kulu, Bilaspur etc. under the patronage of their respective rulers.

Krishna legend was a very popular subject with the Pahari painters. Episodes from Krishna's life were illustrated against the background of beautiful Pahari landscapes. Besides themes taken from mythological legends and epics like the **Ramayana**, the **Mahabharata**, the **Bhagavata Purana**, the **Krishna Lila** and the **Gita-Govinda**, some very interesting paintings of Devi were also painted. **Nayaka-Nayika** themes, portraits, huntings scenes, toilet scenes and festivals such as Holi, love stories namely **Madhu Malti** and **Nala - Damyanti** were also frequently illustrated.

Both male and female costumes in Pahari paintings were influenced by the fashions adopted at the Mughal court from time to time. Nevertheless, there were also distinctive Pahari costumes, particularly those worn by females and they are quite visible in these paintings.

The Basohli School is the oldest one amongst Pahari Schools in the hill area. There is no evidence of any Pahari painting earlier than the reign of Kirpal Pal. The work of some itinerant artist of Mughal School visiting the hill states to execute commissions should not be confused with Pahari paintings. The distinctive style of Basohli with its primitive vitality emerged in the last quarter of the 18th century under Raja Kripal Pal. It is characterised by vivid and bold colours. Faces in the early Basohli paintings are oval in shape with receding foreheads and large expressive eyes like lotus petals.

The landscape is stylised and trees are often depicted in circular form. The composition is simple but unique. Sometimes, a section and figures of the architecture are placed separately into a square frame indicating a true understanding of space sense. The Basohli Style spread over the neighbouring states remained in vogue till the middle of the 18th century. A popular theme in Basohli painting particularly during the reign of Kripal Pal was the **Rasamanjari** written by the poet Bhanu Datta, a Maithili Brahmin, who lived in the 16th century in an area called Tirhut in Bihar. A **Basohli Rasamanjari** series dated 1695 is a landmark. It was illustrated by Devidas, a local painter of Basholi belonging to the Tarkhan community, which produced many skilled aritsans. Amongst other styles of Pahari painting, those of Guler and Kangra, are marked by far more naturalistic treatment of figures and landscapes than seen in Basohli paintings. The figures which are well-modelled and naturalistic are painted in soft and harmonious colours. Whereas paintings of Garhwal school, developed from the Kangra style, show an extensive use of leafless trees, the Kulu Style has folk elements with squarish and somewhat ungainly figures.

14

The Nurpur paintings are characterised by tall women who have long limbs particularly below the waist and are always elegantly attired. The Chamba Style is similar to that of Guler paintings as several artists of this school came from Guler. In Mandi School, we again find some folk elements particularly in the work done during the reign of Raja Shamsher Singh. While Bilaspur also had a style of its own, which extended to Sirmur, the work at Jammu was dominated by the masterly and expressive draughtsmanship of the Nainsukh whose patron was Raja Balwant Singh of Jammu, who is portrayed extensively in Nainsukh paintings in all walks of life. Nainsukh was the master-artist of Jammu school just as his elder brother Manak was of Guler school. Both were sons of Pandit Sen of Guler. The family of Pandit Sen is known for a number of noted artists who worked in various Pahari states developing their own styles. After the death of Goverdhan Chand of Guler in 1773, Manak, his two sons Kaushala and Paltu and his nephew Godhu worked at the court of his successor Prakash Chand till circa A.D. 1785. Prakash Chand, a great lover of arts had spent so lavishly by that time that he became a bankrupt. Thereafter, Manak with his sons and nephew joined the court of Raja Sansar Chand, paramount ruler of the hills, and painted there five sets of paintings during 1785 and 1795. They are: the famous **Bhagavat Purana**, a beautiful **Ramayana** series, a **Satsai** series painted as we know by Paltu, a **Ragamala** now in the National Gallery of Modern Art, New Delhi and a **Baramasa** in the possession of the descendants of Sansar Chand (Lambagaon family). The style of these sets as the work of Manak, his sons and nephew is remarkable and these sets are amongst the greatest achievements of Pahari paintings.

The processes and techniques followed by the artists were almost uniform, simple and indigenous. Handmade paper was mainly used as the base of the paintings. Thin sheets of paper, were joined together to get the requisite thickness, on which the outline was drawn in the light reddish brown or grey-black colour. A thin transparent white coating was applied to the paper. Thereafter, a final drawing was made over the white coating and then the colours were filled in. The pigments were obtained from minerals and vegetables which were suspended in water with gum, for the latter acted as a binding medium. Squirrel and camel hair were used in brushes. Quite often, the painting was burnished, with glass or agate or stone from the river Beas called 'Golla' to obtain the quality of brightness.

I
KRISHNA AND GOPIS
Bihari Sat Sai
Mewar, Rajasthan, circa A.D. 1700
Acc. No. 49.19/59
National Museum, New Delhi

III
SAINT MUSICIAN SWAMI HARIDAS,
AKBAR AND TANSEN
Kishangarh, Rajasthan, circa A.D. 1760
Acc. No. 4814/61
National Museum, New Delhi

II
LAILA MAJNU
Kota, Rajasthan, circa A.D. 1760-70
Acc. No. 56.136/12
National Museum, New Delhi

IV
KRISHNA KILLING BAKASURA
Bhagavata Purana, Guler
Pahari, circa A.D. 1760-1765
Acc. No. 58.18/6
National Museum, New Delhi

V ➪
TODI RAGINI
Pratapgarh, Rajasthan, circa A.D. 1710
Acc. No. 59.29/9
National Museum, New Delhi

VI
KRISHNA RAISING MOUNT
GOVARDHAN
Pahari, circa A.D. 1700
Acc. No. 65.161
National Museum, New Delhi

VII
KHAMBHAVATI RAGINI
Malwa, A.D. 1660

22

23

VIII
NEWLY WEDDED BRIDE
Jaipur, Rajasthan, circa A.D. 1780
Acc. No. 49.19/294
National Museum, New Delhi

24

Line Drawings

Turbans in Pahari Paintings

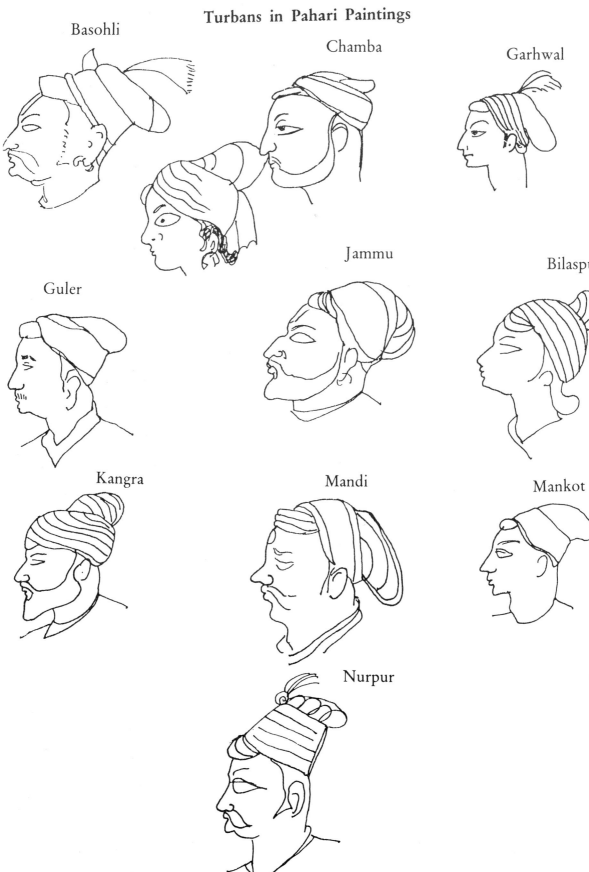

Basohli

Chamba

Garhwal

Guler

Jammu

Bilaspur

Kangra

Mandi

Mankot

Nurpur

Different faces and turbans in Rajasthani Paintings

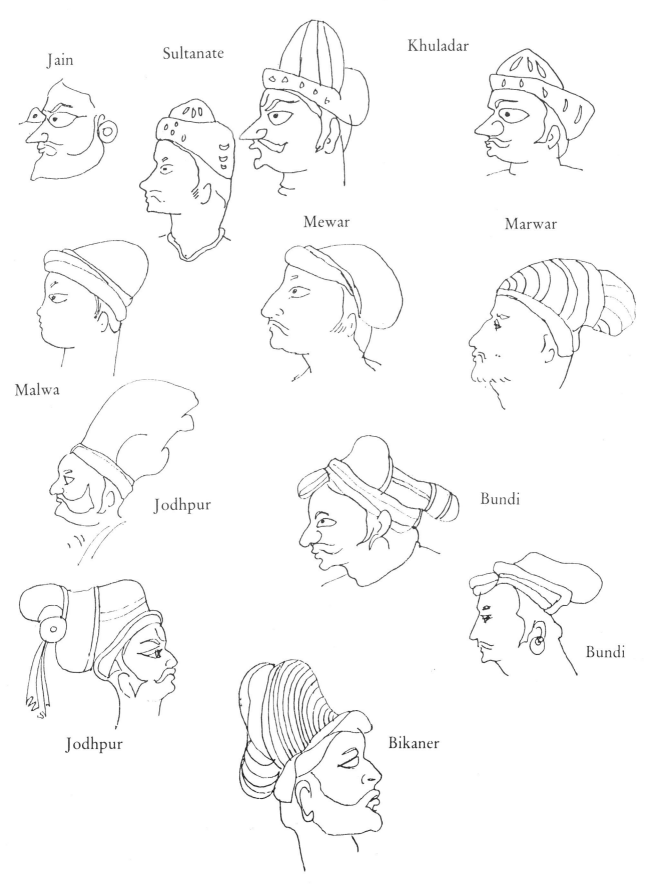

Jain

Sultanate

Khuladar

Mewar

Marwar

Malwa

Jodhpur

Bundi

Jodhpur

Bikaner

Bundi

27

Different faces in Pahari Paintings

Basohli

Chamba

Garhwal

Guler

Jammu

Kangra

Kangra

Different faces in Rajasthani Paintings

Jain

Khuladar

Sultanate

Early Malwa

Malwa

Mewar

Jodhpur

Bikaner

Bundi

Kota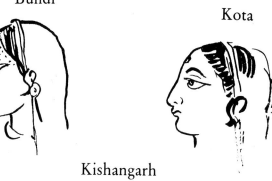

Kishangarh

Architectural designs of various schools

Khuladar

Sultanate

Sultanate

Khuladar

Malwa

Malwa

Malwa

Malwa

Malwa

Bundi

Kota

Mewar

Kota

Ahmadnagar

Different dresses in the Paintings

Jain   Khuladar   Sultanate

Mewar   Mewar

Malwa

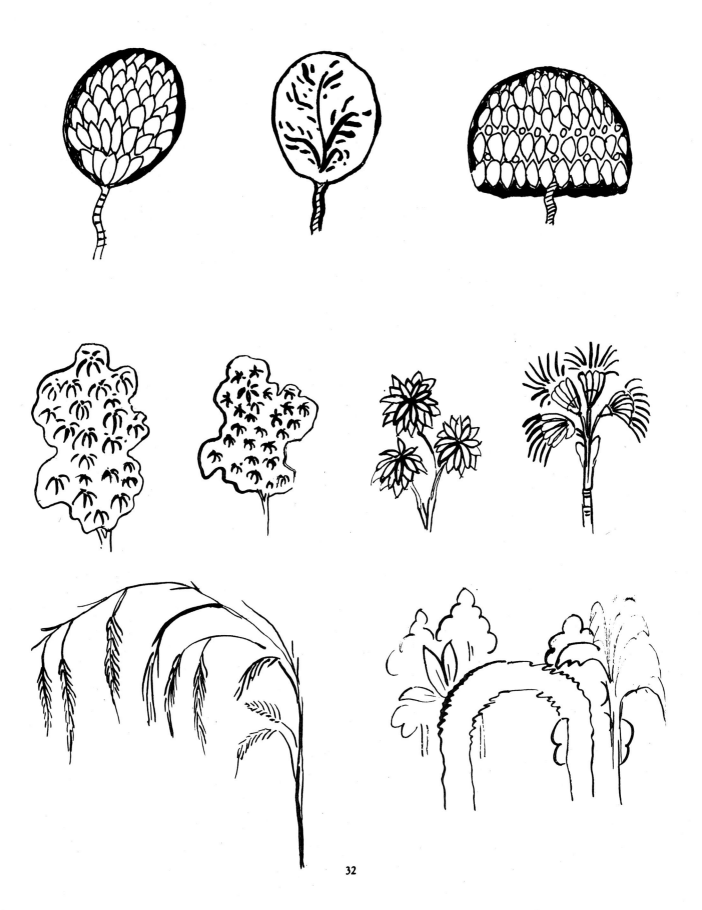

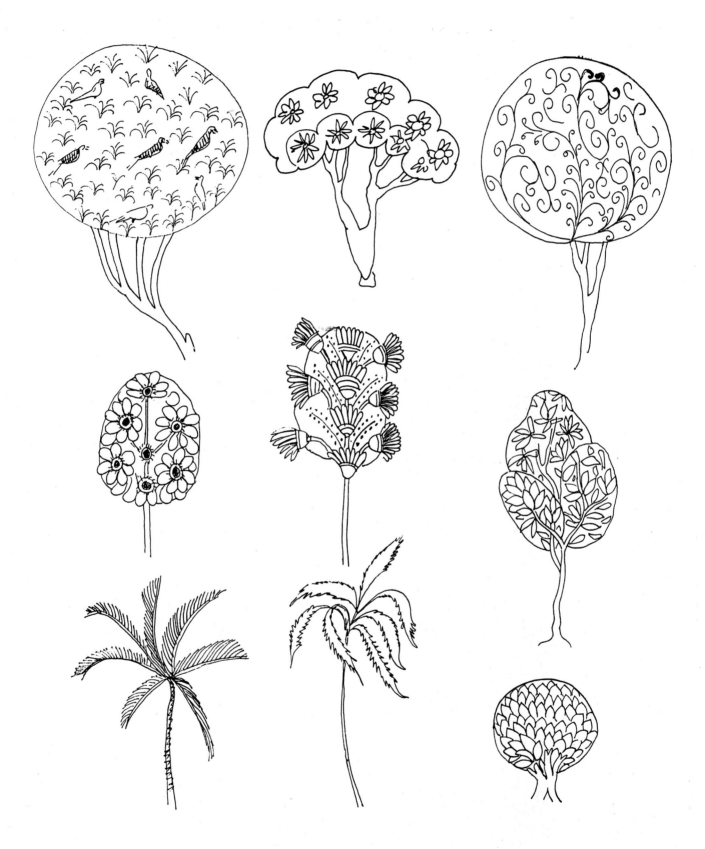

Monochrome Plates

1
MOTHERS OF TIRTHANKARAS
Western Indian School, A.D.–1475-1500
An illustrated leaf from Kalpasutra
(a Jain religious text)
Acc. No. 48.18/1
National Museum, New Delhi

2
KRISHNA WITH GOPIS (Milk Maids)
Western Indian School, A. D. 1450-1475
A leaf from Balgopal Stuti
Acc. No. 60.1655
National Museum, New Delhi

3
A FOLIO FROM BHAGAVATA
Khuladar Style, A. D. 1500-50
Acc. No. 63. 1597
National Museum, New Delhi

4
A PRINCE EXAMINING THE PORTRAIT
OF A LADY
Based on the Tutinama
Mughal Persian
Acc. No. 52.25/2
National Museum, New Delhi

5
AKBAR HUNTING DEER
Mughal, Late 16th century
Acc. No. 8.15
National Museum, New Delhi

6
STUDY OF A FALCON
Attributed to Mansur
Mughal School, circa A.D. 1615
Acc. No. 58.20/19
National Museum, New Delhi

7 ⇨
A FOLIO FROM RASIKAPRIYA
Malwa School, A.D. 1634
Acc. No. 49.19/24
National Museum, New Delhi

अथ आरजटीकेसरजामहि दूरस नरवीजसकु
जानिआरनटीआरसुतहपरसेयद्वरमकवर्षानिआ
बोरघनेद्वानबोरतसजलउलेलके तलकीसन्चिरा
वेफूलफिरेछनसेनजयावक्षेसावनकीपष्ठतीति

चिपंत्खोवहूंकुदनडितातरखैविनिताउरखैक
हिकेसवसावैंजानिमनोवजराडविनाउजळ
परकालकुदुंविनिनोच्चैआशा ॥ ॥

8
A FOLIO FROM BHAGAVATA
Malwa School
Acc. No. 59.205/1
National Museum, New Delhi

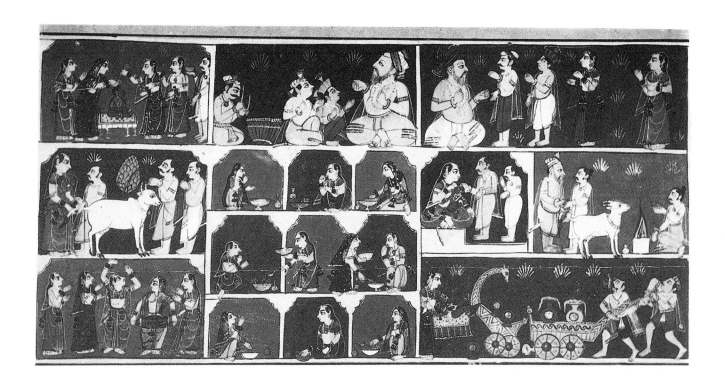

9
A FOLIO FROM RAMAYANA
Malwa School, circa A.D. 1680
Acc. No. 51.65/6
National Museum, New Delhi

10
A FOLIO FROM DHOLA– MARU
By Sahibdin
Mewar School, circa A.D. 1628
Acc. No. 51.52/7
National Museum

ललीत चैरवकोंरगणी॥ ॥प्रफुल्ल...छदमालधरीं युवाचगेरोल्ल संलोचनश्री
विनीसरन बासगृहींता प्रनाने विलानेबोललितप्रदीशा ॥५॥

11
LALITA RAGINI
By Sahibdin
Mewar School, A.D. 1640
Acc. No. 63.1623
National Museum, New Delhi

⇨

12
RAS MANDAL
Mewar School, A.D. 1625-50
Acc. No. 63.162/9
National Museum, New Delhi

॥जिननिस्रितेनिस्रिरतनिस्रारबकौकान्हनिस्रारजिनकेसहनिस्रारक्षु
तनावक्कन्यानकैवालबैपतिवतानक्रकेदियनविहारहैशहिविश्र
रावरहैप्रसेवआगवदफानवपूजीविश्रपचिविारैहैकृष्णमदमोचनमदनमद
नकिवियवतमोचनकिलोचननिस्रारहैंॱॱॱ॥

45

13
BHADRA MASA
(August-September)
Jodhpur, Rajasthan
circa A.D. 1750
Acc. No. 51/210/11
National Museum, New Delhi

46

14
BHADRAPADA
(August-September)
Baramasa, Jodhpur, Rajasthan
circa A.D. 1750
Acc. No. 69.12
National Museum, New Delhi

47

48

15
RADHA AND KRISHNA
Kishangarh, middle 18th Century
Acc. No. 63.1768
National Museum, New Delhi

16
BOAT OF LOVE
Kishangarh, middle 18th century
Acc. No. 63.793
National Museum, New Delhi

17
KRISHNA STEALING BUTTER
Bikaner, A.D. 1740
Acc. No. 72.239
National Museum, New Delhi

⇨
18
LADY AT TOILET
Bundi School, A.D. 1750-75
Acc. No. 51.220/20
National Museum, New Delhi

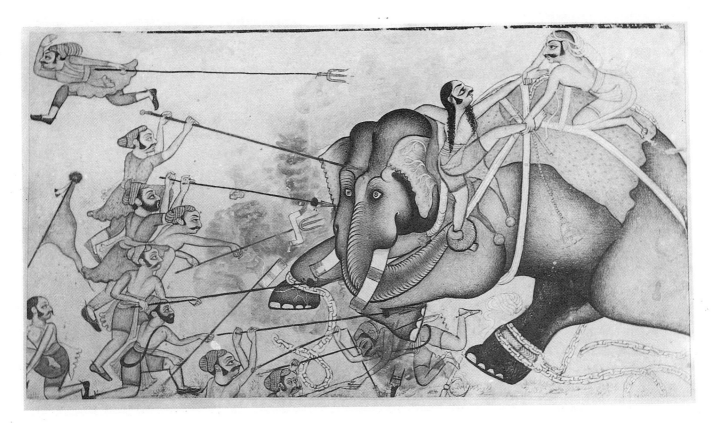

19
A RUN AWAY ELEPHANT
Bundi School, circa A.D. 1800
Acc. No. 63.1670
National Museum, New Delhi

20
LADIES HUNTING TIGERS
Bundi School, circa A.D. 1760
Acc. No. 47.110/1919
National Museum, New Delhi

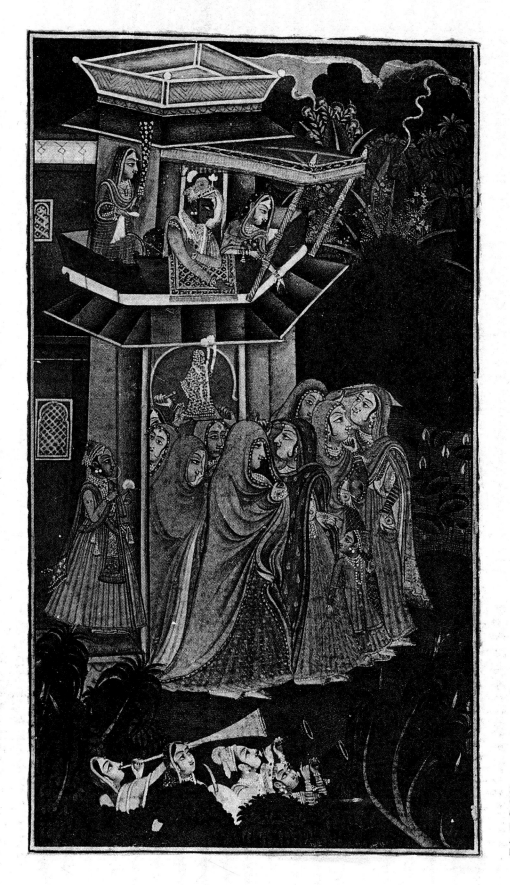

21
CELEBRATION OF THE FESTIVAL
OF GANGAUR
Bundi, A.D. 1750-75
Acc. No. 56.36/24
National Museum, New Delhi

22
MEETING OF LOVERS IN RAIN
Based on Bhumidata's Rasamanjari
Basohli, Pahari, circa A.D. 1695
Acc. No. 47.110/324
National Museum, New Delhi

23
LAKSHMI–NARAYANA ON SHESH SHAIYA
Basohli School, circa A.D. 1725
Acc. No. 62.2458
National Museum, New Delhi

24
A FOLIO FROM GITA-GOVINDA
Basohli School, A.D. 1730
Acc. No. 51.207/13
National Museum, New Delhi

26
KRISHNA PLAYING HOLI WITH GOPIS
Kangra School, circa, A.D. 1780
Acc. No. 51.207
National Museum, New Delhi

25
KRISHNA TAKING TOLL TAX FROM GOPIS
Guler School, circa, A.D. 1770
Acc. No. 71.147
National Museum, New Delhi

27
LADY AT TRYST
Garhwal, Pahari, circa A.D. 1800
Acc. No. 59.27/16
National Museum, New Delhi

28
RADHA–KRISHNA LOOKING
INTO MIRROR
Garhwal, Late 18th century
Acc. No. 49.19/129
National Museum, New Delhi

61

29
KRISHNA PLAYING FLUTE
Kulu, Pahari, circa A.D. 1800
National Museum, New Delhi

⇨
30
RAGA HINDOL
Ahmadnagar, circa, A.D. 1590
B.K.N. 2066
National Museum, New Delhi

31
RAGINI PATHANSANI
Bijapur A.D. 1590-1600
B.K.N. 2063
National Museum, New Delhi